Charles William Darling

New Amsterdam, New Orange, New York

With Chronological Data

Charles William Darling

New Amsterdam, New Orange, New York
With Chronological Data

ISBN/EAN: 9783337415495

Printed in Europe, USA, Canada, Australia, Japan

Cover: Foto ©ninafisch / pixelio.de

More available books at **www.hansebooks.com**

New Amsterdam,

New Orange,

New York,

WITH CHRONOLOGICAL DATA.

—BY—

CHARLES W. DARLING.

Cor. Sec'y of the Oneida Historical Society, Utica, N. Y.

· ● ·

PRIVATELY PRINTED.
1889.

PREFATORY REMARKS.

The historical notes herein given convey an idea of the city of New York as it appeared in its earliest days. They have been gathered, to a large extent, from the writings of De Vries, Denton, Brodhead, De Witt, Benson, Rogers, Bryant, Stevens and Winsor; also from manuscript folio volumes of public records; a portion of which was published by Moulton in 1825. The Knickerbocker authors have furnished much valuable information on this same topic, still something has been left untold.

It is the object of this compilation to fill, in part at least, this vacancy. The notes date back to the period when trading and fishing huts were first erected upon Manhattan Island; they therefore necessarily embrace the years between the discovery of this land by Hudson in 1609, and the recall of Gov. Wouter Van Twiller in 1637.

C. W. D.

These portraitures represent Gen. George and Martha Washington at the time of his inauguration as President of the United States, April 30, 1789.

They are reproductions of the miniatures on ivory, taken from life by the Scotch artist, Mr. Archibald Robertson; and were first given to the public through Mrs. Martha J. Lamb's Magazine of American History, April, 1888.

The originals are owned by the granddaughters of the artist, Mrs. Charles W. Darling and Mrs. S. Matilda Mygatt, and have been deposited on loan, at the request of Gen. L. P. Di Cesnola and others; in the Metropolitan Museum of Art, New York.

Charles W. Darling,

COR. SEC. ONEIDA HISTORICAL SOCIETY, UTICA, N. Y.

Hon. Mem. Alabama Historical Society, Tuscaloosa, Ala.; New Jersey Historical Society, Newark, N. J.; Iowa State Historical Society, Iowa City, Iowa. Cor. Mem. American Numismatic and Archæological Society, New York City, N. Y.; American Ethnological Society, New York City, N. Y.; New York Academy of Anthropology, New York City, N. Y.; Buffalo Historical Society, Buffalo, N. Y.; Chautauqua Society of History and Natural Science, Jamestown, N. Y.; Bangor Historical Society, Bangor, Me.; New Hampshire Historical Society, Concord, New Hamp.; Middlebury Historical Society, Middlebury, Ver.; New England Historic Genealogical Society, Boston, Mass.; Newport Genealogical Society, Newport, R. I.; New Haven Colony Historical Society, New Haven, Conn.; Fairfield County Historical Society, Bridgeport, Conn.; State Archaeological and Historical Society, Columbus, Ohio; Numismatic and Antiquarian Society, Philadelphia, Pa.; Wyoming Historical and Geological Society, Wilkes Barre, Pa.; Linnæan, Scientific and Historical Society, Lancaster, Pa.; Historical and Geological Society, Indianapolis, Ind.; Maryland Historical Society, Baltimore, Md.; Virginia Historical Society, Richmond, Va.; Georgia Historical Society, Savannah, Ga.; Tennessee Historical Society, Nashville, Tenn.; Wisconsin State Historical Society, Madison, Wis.; Minnesota Historical Society, St. Paul, Minn.; Kansas Historical Society, Topeka, Kan.; Nebraska Historical Society, Lincoln, Neb.; California Historical Society, Berkeley, Cal.; American Historical Association. Resident member of the New York Historical Society, 1862. Col and Aid-de-Camp to Gov. E. D. Morgan, S.N.Y., 1859–60; Col. and Aid-de-Camp on the Staff of Maj. Gen. B. F. Butler, Corps Comd'r. Army of the James, 1864; Col. and A. A. Paymaster-Gen. and State Agent 1865 6; Brig. Gen. and Com. Gen. of Subsistence, S.N.Y. 1866; Brig. Gen. and Mil. Eng-in-Chief, S.N.Y. 1867-8; Com'r of the State of Conn., 1866–71.

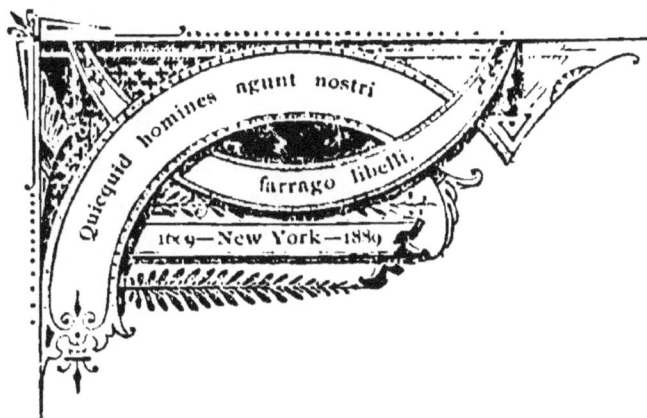

Quicquid homines agunt nostri
farrago libelli.
1609—New York—1889

THE Rev. Thomas De Witt, D.D., (of blessed memory,) in an historical discourse delivered August, 1856, stated that the Protestant Reformed Dutch Church of New York City, the first founded in North America, dates from about the time of the first settlement on Manhattan Island. After the discovery of the island in 1609, commercial adventures were made by Holland merchants, and small trading ports were formed at Manhattan and Fort Orange as early as 1613. It was not until after the formation of the West India Company in 1621, that measures were taken for an agricultural settlement in New Netherland, in 1623. Among the small number of these early settlers were some Walloons, who, during the severity of the religious persecution in the seventeenth century, had fled from the French Belgic provinces to Holland, and had become domesticated there. The first born white child was the daughter of George Janse D'Rapalje, one of these same Walloon settlers, who located on the Long Island shore at Walleboght. It was stipulated by the West India Company, whenever emigrants went forth under their auspices, and that of the States-General of Holland, to send with them a school master a pious member of the church, whose office should be to instruct the children, and preside at religious meetings until the regular ministry should be over them. The ziekentroosters (comforters of the sick,) were commissioned as assistants to the ministers of the gospel; and in 1626 Governor Minuit came to America with two individuals, who were to act in this capacity. During this year, as the records show, Minuit purchased from the aborigines the entire island of Manhattan, then estimated to contain about 22,000 acres of land, for the value of 60 guilders, or about $24 of our present currency, when it was ceded by the native proprietors to the Dutch West India Company. For a time, the religious meetings of those grand old Dutch pioneers were held in temporary buildings, and it is in evidence that as early as 1626, a congregation met in a spacious room over a horse-mill, owned or occupied by Francois Molemaker. After the arrival of Dominie Bogardus in 1633, a plain wooden building was erected, situate on the East River, near what is now Old Slip. Here the services were conducted until 1642, when David Peterson de Vriez, the famous navigator, and Governor William Kieft secured the appointment of a committee to procure the needed funds from individuals, and from the West India Company, for the building of a suitable church edifice. The call was as promptly and as willingly responded to by those noble sires, as similar calls are met by the representative Dutchmen of to-day; and before the close of the same year a Reformed Dutch Church was erected within the fort, at its south-east corner. It was built of stone, and covered with shingles, which, from their exposure to the weather, soon resembled slate.

Jochem Pietersz Kuyter and Jan Claesz Damen were elected to serve with David Pietersz Vriez and William Kieft, as the first consistory of the "Gereformeerde Kerck," or Reformed Dutch church. This name, given in 1529 in the parent land, arose when six princes of the German empire formally and solemnly protested against the decrees of the Diet Spires, and it has since been the distinctive name, as applied to the glorious Reformation.

The late Rev. E. P. Rogers, D.D., in a sermon preached in the North Dutch Church Nov. 26, 1857, thus alludes to the name, doctrinal standards, and polity of the Reformed Dutch Church. "They are derived from the action of those who met at Antwerp in 1563, and adopted a system of principles and rules which laid the foundation, and in a great measure formed the full texture of church government and order adopted by subsequent synods. We bear a name connected with the grandest historical associations and noblest memories of the past. It associates us with some of the brightest names in the catalogue of God's illustrious servants. It dates back to the time when, at the command of God, the light of the Reformation illumined the dark ages, and brought freedom to imprisoned souls. It connects us with such illustrious names as Luther, Calvin, Knox, Cranmer, Wessel, Gansevoort, Rudolph, Agricola and others, who, as Demarest says in his history of the Reformed Protestant Dutch Church, sowed the seed which was quickened into life by the Reformation. The mother church was distinguished in that day for the profound, learning of her theologians, the devotion of her pastors, the purity of her creed, and the scriptural beauty of her forms of worship. She opened her arms freely to welcome the fugitive Huguenot, the out-lawed Jew, and the exiled Puritan. She sheltered in her bosom the wanderer from the valleys of Piedmont, and the mountains of Scotland. She had drank of the bitter cup of persecution, and the sufferer for conscience sake, though a stranger to her land and her dialect, was ever hailed as a brother in their common Lord.

Such are the associations connected with the name and origin of this early church; and it is pleasant, also, to think that those noble men who landed on Plymouth Rock, and to whom this Western world owes so much, came from their own land by the way of Holland, where for twelve years they found a safe retreat from persecution, and enjoyed the Christian hospitality of their Dutch brethren. That twelve years of sojourn in the Netherlands might have been no unimportant portion of the training of the Pilgrims for the work which lay before them on the rocky shores of New England. The Reformed Churches of Germany, Scotland, France, Switzerland and Holland, when the Reformation from Popery took rise, were in close affinity with each other, not only in holding the doctrines of grace, but in their views of the Lord's Supper, and also of Presbyterian church government and order.

The contract made by the men who composed the first consistory of the old Dutch Church within the fort is upon record. It was made in May, 1642, before the Secretary of the New Netherlands, between William Kieft, at the request of his brethren, the wardens of the church in New Netherland, John Ogden of Stanford and Richard Ogden, who contracted to build the church of rock stone, 70 feet long, 52 broad, and 16 feet high above the soil, for twenty-five hundred guilders, (£416.13 4,) "in beaver, cash or merchandise, to-wit: if the church wardens are satisfied with the work, so that in their judgment the 2,500 guilders shall have been earned, then said church wardens will reward them with one hundred guilders ($£$16.13 4,) more; in the meantime, assist them whenever it is in their power, and allow them the use, for a month or six weeks, of the company's boat, to facilitate the carrying of the stone thither."

The church was not completely finished until the first year of Governor Stuyvesant's administration. In July, 1647, he and two others were appointed kerk meesters, (church wardens,) to superintend the work and complete it during the winter.

This continued to be their house of worship until the church in Garden street was opened in 1693 for service. In form, this edifice was an oblong square, with three sides of an octagon on the east side. In the front, on a large square foundation, it had a brick steeple, and the interior space above the entrance was used as a consistory room. The window sashes contained small panes of glass set in lead, many of which had upon them the coats of arms of those who had been elders and magistrates, curiously burnt on glass by Gerard Duyckinck. This building continued the only house of worship for the Dutch people until another edifice was erected at the corner of Nassau and Liberty streets. The Garden street church was called the *Old*, the Nassau street the *New*, and when the church at the corner of Fulton and William was erected, it took the name of the *North*. Then the Garden street church was designated as the *South*, and the Nassau street as the *Middle*.

At the front entrance of the old church in the fort, was placed a stone with this inscription: "An. Dom. MDCXLII, W. Kieft Dir. Gen. Heeft de Gemeente dese tempel doen bouwen." In the year of our Lord, one thousand six hundred and forty-two, W. Kieft, being director-general, has this congregation caused this temple to be built. In 1790, when the foundations of the fort were being dug away, this stone was found among the rubbish. It was removed to the church in Garden street, where it remained until both were destroyed in the great fire of December, 1835.

The baptismal and other records of the Reformed Dutch church commence in 1639, and appear in the hand writing of Dominie Selyns, who carefully arranged them. All previous records were probably destroyed at a remote period of time.

The colony of New Netherland remained forty years after the first agricultural settlement, when, in 1664, the land was ceded to the British Government by a treaty which secured to the Dutch their ecclesiastical and civil privileges. During the administration of Gov. Stuyvesant, the colony had grown considerably, and the population of New Amsterdam at the time of the session was about sixteen hundred. Dominie Selyns preached at Brooklyn and Gov. Stuyvesant's bouwerie, from 1660 to 1664, when he returned to Holland. On the decease of the ministers Drisius and Megapolensis, the church of New York sent a call to Selyns in Holland, which he declined, but subsequently, after the death of Van Nieuwenhuysen, the call having been renewed, was accepted. In 1682 he became sole pastor of the church, and continued such until the year 1699, when Rev. Gualterus Dubois became his associate.

Referring to subjects connected with the city proper, and its inhabitants, it may be well to state that in August, 1673, while England was at war with Holland, a fleet belonging to the latter, and commanded by commodores Cornelis Evertsen and Jacob Benches; captains Anthonio Colve, Nicolaes Boes, and Ab. Fierd. Van Zyll recaptured New York. Exercising the power of a supreme military tribunal, they named the city New Orange, in compliment to the Dutch prince of Orange. Pursuant to a treaty of peace between England and Holland, that closed the war in 1674, New Orange was re-delivered to the English, who gave it the name by which it has since been distinguished. At the remarkable era when the Dutch were in possession of the city, the legislative, executive and judicial power was vested in the governor and his council. The hoofd-schout (high sheriff,) acted as fiscael, (attorney-general,) and conducted offenders to the gaol, whipping post, wooden horse, gallows, or transport ship. If a criminal was guilty of *crimen lesae majestatis*, or of libel on the burgomasters, he was led to a stake with a bridle in his mouth, rods under his arm, and a label on his breast. The weesmeesters had charge of the poor, and the roymeesters regulated the fences, and the citizens were divided into two classes; the groot burgerrecht and klein burgerrecht.

The amusements and customs of the people consisted in dancing the hipsey-saw, shuffle-shuffle, playing cards, nine-pins, and trick-track; plucking the goose, planting the may-pole, surrounded with ragged stockings, sailing to Nut (Governor's) Island or Brenkelen. Walks were taken to the Ladies' Valley, (Maiden Lane,) and rides to the Bouwerie, Corlear's Hook, Sapokanikan, Bloemend 'Dal, Nieuw Harlaem, Spyt den Duyvel Kill, or Vreedendal, (Westchester.)

Anthonio Colve was commissioned as governor, under the provisional sanction of the States-General and the Prince of Orange. Cornelis Steenwyck was appointed as his counselor-of-state, and Nicholas Bayard as Secretary of New Netherlands. Jacobus Van de Water was made auditor of the Military Council, and the burgomasters and schepens took their position in line. A code of sanguinary military law was deemed necessary, and the strictest discipline in garrison and among the militia was enforced. The mayor, at the head of the latter, held his daily parades before the City Hall, and each evening he received from the hoofd-wagt (guard) of the fort the keys, with which, (accompanied by a sergeant and six armed soldiers,) he locked the city gates. The burger-wagt (citizen on guard,) opened the gates at daylight, and returned the keys to the commanding officer at the fort. During this interval no person could go upon the ramparts, bulwarks, rondeels or batteries of the city, on pain of corporal punishment; but if any individual dared to enter or leave the city except through the gate, death was the penalty. At the fort the soldiers were daily paraded and exercised, the guard mounted the ramparts upon duty, the sentinels were stationed at the gates, the *reveille* was played each morning at daybreak, the *tap-toe* beaten each evening at 9 o'clock, and the daily discharges of musketry and occasional roar of artillery were heard in echoes at Flatten Barrack, Golden and Potbaker's Hills, or in reverberation along the surrounding shores and forests. Every day a corporal's guard was on duty from each company in garrison, when the muskets were examined. At night the corporals changed their sentinels each half hour, and the hoofd-rond (chief round) went before midnight and received the password. During the day the corporals changed their sentinels as circumstances required. Their further duty was to see that muskets were cleaned and well charged, to examine the ammunition and bandeliers, (cartridge boxes,) to keep their men in or near the guard-house, and to prevent the introduction of liquor. A code of military law was read aloud by the corporal every time the soldiers went on guard, so that no one might pretend ignorance. By this code, they were liable to be punished for blasphemy with confinement on bread and water three days; for a second offense, the tongue was perforated with a hot iron. Death was decreed for mutiny, for leaving his *corps de garde* without permission, for challenging to fight, for opposition to his officers, or to be found sleeping when on duty. Whoever became intoxicated during guard was cashiered and banished from the company. He who did not appear on parade, received punishment by being placed on the wooden horse. One of the first acts of the military tribunal was to invite the citizens to assemble and appoint a committee of six, to confer with the council. At the conference, these six deputies received a request to call a meeting of the citizens to nominate six persons for burgomasters, and fifteen for schepens, "of the best and most respectable citizens of the reformed christian religion only." By a majority of votes the citizens nominated for burgomasters were Cornelis Steenwyck, Cornelis Van Ruyven, Johannis Van Brugh, Marten Cregier, Johannis de Peyster, and Nicholas Bayard; for schepens, Jeronimus Ebbingh, William Beeckman,

Egidius Luyck, Jacob Kip, Gelyn Verplanck, Lourans Van de Spiegel, Balthazaer Bayard, Francois Rombouts, Stephen Van Cortlant, Adolph Pietersen, Reynier Willemsen, Peter Jacobsen, Jan Vigne, Pieter Stoutenburg and Coenract Ten Eyck.

They took an oath of allegiance to the high and mighty lords, the States-General of the United Netherlands, and his highness, the lord prince of Orange, to obey their magistrates, administer equal justice, promote the welfare of the city, and defend the true christian religion, in conformity to the Synod of Dordrecht, as instructed in the churches of Netherland. On the 13th of August a proclamation was issued restoring the form of the government of the city to its ancient character, as practiced in the Fatherland, and the officers commissioned were directed in addition to the duties indicated by their oath, to govern the inhabitants, citizens and strangers, "in conformity to the laws and statutes of Holland." The commission for governor bore date the 17th September. After he and his council were left in the full exercise of supreme legislation, executive and judicial authority, they issued the following instructions:

Instructions for Jacobus Van de Water, as mayor and auditor of the city of New Orange.

1. The mayor shall take good care that in the morning the gates are opened at sunrise, and

locked again in the evening with sunset; for which purpose he shall go to the principal guard, and there address himself to the commanding officer, and demand to conduct him thither, at least a sergeant with six soldiers, (schutters,) all armed with guns. With these he shall proceed to the fort to fetch the keys, and return these again there as soon as the gates are opened or shut. There he shall receive the watch-word from the governor, or from the officer commanding in his absence, when he shall again return to the city hall, and deliver the received orders to the sergeant of the guard.

2. The mayor shall be present at all military tribunals, and have his vote in his turn, next the youngest ensign.

3. The mayor may every night make the round, give the watch-word to the corporal, visit the guards, and if there are some absent, make the next day his report to the governor.

4. As auditor, he shall act in the military council as secretary, and take care that a correct register is kept of all the transactions. This book (notules,) shall remain under the care of the auditor—and deliver no copy of it, except upon special orders.

Done at Fort Willem Hendrick, 12 Jan., 1674.

Provisional instructions for the sheriff, burgomasters and schepens, of the city of New Orange.

1. The sheriff and magistrates shall, each in their quality, take proper care that the reformed

Christian religion, in conformity to the synod of Dordrecht, is maintained—without permitting that any thing contrary to it shall be attempted by any other sect.

2. The sheriff shall be present at all meetings, and then preside, except that his honour the governor, or any other person commissioned by him, was present, who in such case shall preside, when the sheriff shall follow the youngest burgomaster. But whenever the sheriff is acting in behalf of justice, or in any other manner as plaintiff, then in such case he shall, after having made his conclusion, rise from his seat and absent himself from the bench during the decision.

3. All cases relative to the police, security, and peace of the inhabitants—so too of justice between man and man, shall be determined by definite sentences by the schout, burgomasters and schepens, to the amount of fifty beavers and below it; but in all cases exceeding that sum, all persons are free to appeal to the governor-general and council here.

4. All criminal delicts committed here within the city and its jurisdiction, shall be judged by the aforesaid sheriff, burgomasters and schepens, who shall have power to sentence and judge even punishment of death—provided that all judgments and corporal punishments shall not be executed before these are approved by the governor-general and his council, this approbation being demanded and obtained.

5. The meetings shall be convocated by the president burgomaster, which he shall communicate the day before to captain Willem Knyff, who by this is provisionally authorized and qualified to be present at the meetings, and preside in them in the name and in the behalf of the governor, and so too the sheriff, burgomasters and schepens.

6. All proposals shall be made by the first burgomaster, which proposal being made, then shall upon it the first advice be given by him who presides in the name of the governor, and so of course by the remaining magistrates, each in his rank; and after the collection of votes, it shall by the majority be concluded. But if it happen that the votes are equal, then the president may conclude with his vote, in which case those of the contrary opinion, or the minority, may have their opinion placed on the protocol, but may not divulge it in public, under the penalty of an arbitrary correction.

7. The burgomasters shall change their rank each half year, when the oldest shall be first president, and he who follow him the next; but for this year the change shall be every fourth month, because this year three burgomasters have been appointed.

8. The sheriff, burgomasters and schepens, shall hold their sessions as often as it may be required, provided they determine on fixed days.

9. The sheriff, burgomasters and schepens, are authorized to resolve for the benefit, tranquillity

and peace of the inhabitants of their district, and publish and fix, with the approbation of the governor, any statutes, ordinances and placards; provided that they are not contrary, but, as far as it may be possible, agreeing with the laws and statutes of our Fatherland.

10. The said sheriff, burgomasters and schepens, shall be obliged to rigid observance of all the placards and ordinances which are commanded and published by supreme authority, and see that these are executed, and not to permit that any act to the contrary is performed, but that the contraveners are prosecuted in conformity to its contents; and that, further, all such orders shall be promptly executed, which shall be conveyed to them by the governor-general, from time to time.

11. The sheriff, burgomasters and schepens, shall be further obliged to acknowledge their high and mighty lords, the States-General of the United Netherlands, and his serene highness, the lord prince of Orange, as their supreme sovereign, and to maintain their high jurisdiction, rights, and domains in this country.

12. The election of all inferior officers and ministers for the service of the aforesaid sheriff, burgomasters and schepens, the secretary's office only excepted, shall be elected and confirmed by themselves.

13. The sheriff shall carry into execution all sentences of burgomasters and schepens, without releasing any individual except with advice of the Court; and take particular good care that the resort subjected to him, be thoroughly cleansed from all villainies, brothels and similar impurities.

14. The sheriff shall enjoy all the fines during the time of his service, provided that these shall not exceed the sum of twelve hundred guilders, sewant's value, annually; which sum having received, he shall of all the other fines receive the just half, provided that he shall neither directly nor indirectly enter into a compromise with any delinquent, but leave this to the judicature of the magistrates.

15. The sheriff, burgomasters and schepens aforesaid shall on the 11th day of the month of August, being eight days before the election of the new magistrates, call a meeting, and in the presence of a committee chosen for that purpose by the governor-general, nominate a double number of the best qualified, honest and respectable inhabitants, and only such as are of the reformed Christian religion, or who are at least favorable to it, and well affectionate, for sheriff, burgomasters and schepens aforesaid, which nomination that same day shall be sealed and delivered, from which then the election shall be made on the 17th of the month of August, with the continuation of some of the old

magistrates, if it was deemed proper or necessary.
Done in Fort Willem Hendrick 15 Jan., 1674.
By order of the governor-general of Netherland.

N. BAYARD,

(*Signed.*)   *Secretary.*

In August, 1674, the re-election of city officers
took place, "agreeably to custom, and the specific
instructions of the governor."

The old sheriff, burgomasters and schepens
accordingly met at the city hall, the place of their
sessions, and nominated a double list of "the most
respectable and wealthiest inhabitants," viz.:   For
burgomasters—Willem Beeckman, Oloff Stevensen
Cortland.   For schepens—Stephanus Van Cortland,
Francois Rombouts, Jan Vigne, Peter Jacobsen
Marius, Christopher Hoogland, Gerret Van Tricht.
Those elected were Willem Beeckman, Stephanus
Van Cortland, Francois Rombouts, and Christopher
Hoogland.   The others were J. Van Brug, old burgomaster, Jacob Kipp, presiding schepen, and Gelyn
Verplanck, schepen.   At the close of the pre-
ceding year, the expenses incurred in repairing
the fortifications and providing for the public de-
fense, amounted to 11,000 guilders, to meet which a
tax assessment was made upon the people, according
to the capital which the inhabitants possessed. One
hundred and thirty-four estates were taxed, and the
aggregate amount was about £95,000.   Cash was

scarce in the city, and the government officers and others were paid in seawant or beavers. Seawant, or seawan, was the name of Indian money. It was called, also, wampum, and consisted of beads formed of the shells of shell fish. It was of two colors, the black being considered double the value of the white. Its current value was six beads of the white, or three of the black, for an English penny.

At this period of time, the Capsey, or dividing point between the North and East rivers, terminated a short distance south of State street, and was the ancient boundary of the shore. A row of buildings were upon Capsey street, and extended to Whitehall street. Between Pacrel (Pearl) street and the fort stood the large wooden horse about twelve feet high, with an edged back, where persons guilty of misdemeanors were punished. The culprit was seated astride with his legs fastened by a chain to an iron stirrup. Fort Willem Hendrick, the name officially given to the fort in 1673, was commenced in 1635 by Gov. Van Twiller, neglected by Gov. Kieft, repaired by Gov. Stuyvesant, and demolished in 1790-91. It was situated directly south of Bowling Green, on high ground, was in shape of a square with four bastions, two gates and mounted 42 cannon.

The governor's stone house erected by Kieft was 100 feet long, 50 wide, and 24 high, with two outside walks the length of the building, the one nine and the other ten feet broad; entry 50 feet long and 20 broad, with a partition and double chimney. An inferior one was previously built partly of logs and brick upon the same site, by Van Twiller. Stuyvesant's house was built about four years before he surrendered his government to the English. It fronted the public wharf, and stood on the west side of the present Whitehall street, nearly opposite the commencement of the present Water street.

The Secretary's office was at the north gate, near the north-east bastion of the fort.

It was erected in behalf of Cornelis Tienhoven, who was secretary of New Netherland under Van Twiller and Kieft. From this office the first post-rider started, at the commencement of every month on his rounds to Boston, Hartford, and other places along the road.

The proclamation of Gov. Lovelace, issued December 10, 1672, is a document too curious to be omitted. It was in the following words:

"Whereas it is thought convenient, and necessary, in obedience to his Sacred Majesty's Commands, who enjoynes all his subjects, in their distinct colonyes, to enter into a strict Allyance and Correspondency with each other, as likewise for the advancement of Negotiation, Trade, and Civill Commerce, and for a more speedy Intelligence and Dispatch of affayres, that a messenger or Post bee authorised to sett forth from this City of New-Yorke, monthly, and thence to travaile to Boston, from whence within that month hee shall returne againe to this City. These are therefore to give notice to all persons concerned, That on the first day of January next (1673) the messenger appointed shall proceed on his Journey to Boston: If any therefore have any letters or small portable goods to bee conveyed to Hartford, Connecticott, Boston, or any other parts in the Road, they shall bee carefully delivered according to the Directions by a sworne Messenger and Post, who is purposely imployed in that Affayre; In the Interim those that bee dispos'd to send Letters, lett them bring them to the Secretary's office, where is a lockt Box they shall be preserv'd till the Messenger calls for them. All persons paying the Post before the Bagg bee sealed up.

Dated at New Yorke this 10th day of Dec. 1672."

The public wharf and dock were built by the burgomasters of the city about the year 1658. Here vessels were loaded and unloaded, and a wharfage duty was exacted of eight stivers per last. The harbor was constructed to accommodate vessels and yachts, where during winter they might be secure against the floating ice; for which privilege large vessels paid annually to the city "one beaver;" smaller craft in proportion. This wharf and harbor are now a part of Whitehall street, Whitehall slip having since been formed into the river.

The public store-houses, or *pack-huysen* of the Dutch West India Company, the "lords patroons" of this city, were situated in Winckel-straet, (Stone street,) which then extended from the now White-hall street, to Broad street. Between Winckel-straet and the dock, and the wall along the harbor, and in the direction across the bridge, at the foot of Heeren-gracht, was Brug straet, (now Bridge street,) and between this and the dock was that portion of the present continuation of Pearl street, formerly called Dock street. Here a small market house was erected in 1656, and a market established every Saturday on the shore, because farmers, as the order in council recited, "now and then" had brought various articles "as beef, pork, butter, cheese, turnips, carrots, cabbages and other products of the country; and on coming to the shore often waited a great while to their loss, because the commonalty, who resided at some distance from the shore, remained ignorant that such articles were offered for sale."

In rear of Winckle street, and between that and Beever-gracht, (now Beaver street,) was an open space called *markt-velt*, where a market had been held and cattle shows exhibited before the market house on the shore was erected. It embraced the plain before the fort, and a lane reaching from Market-field to Broad street, called Marktvelt-steegje, (Market-field-lane,) afterwards better known as Petticoat-lane. The most westerly buildings bordered on the east side of Breede-weg, or Broadway, which on the west side was carefully left open for the range of the cannon of the fort. Along the west side from the fort, as far as the present Trinity church, was the West India Company's garden, and thence beyond the city walls was the company's farm, afterwards called the King's farm, and extending to the present Duane street. In the time of Gov. Kieft, Broad street, or Heeren-gracht, (gentlemen's canal,) was called the *Moat*, and at the close of the English Governor Lovelace's administration (1672) the *Great Dyke* was cleaned, when also the streets of the city were paved. Many supplies were brought to the town by boats which sailed through the Broad street canal, and were tied to the bridge over the canal at the corner of Bridge and Broad streets. This bridge was used in those early days as the Merchants Exchange.

Four years after (1676) the gracht (canal) was ordered to be filled up, and the street made level and paved. Beever-gracht entered the Heeren-gracht from the west, and Princes-gracht (now a continued part of Beaver street,) extended eastward and terminated in a sloot or ditch, whence was derived the name of Sloat-lane. In the vicinity of the Heeren-gracht was the Schapen-wey, or the sheep pasture, sometimes called the sheep valley. From the Heeren-gracht to the Stadt-huys inclosure, was Hoog-straet, (High street,) that is from a point a

little northwest of the corner of the present Pearl
and Broad streets to the south corner of the lane leading from Coenties-slip into Stone street. The Stadt-
huys or Stadt-herberg was situated at the corner of
Hoog-straet, called afterwards Little Dock street, and
the lane running from Coenties-slip westward into
the street which is now a continuation of Stone
street. It was built by Gov. Kieft and finished in
1642, for the purpose in part of relieving himself
from the burden of hospitality with which he had
been taxed, while his New England neighbors tar-
ried at the "Manhadoes" on their voyages to Virginia. It was erected at the expense of the West
India Company, and was afterwards, upon application of the burgomasters, granted to the city for a
Stadt-Huys, as well as the public tavern. This
celebrated building, in which the most memorable
affairs of the colony were discussed, and sometimes
transacted; in which the schout burgomasters and
schepens held their sessions and courts; in which
the transfer of the sovereignty over the city and
colony from one power to another was three times
agitated and acceded to; in which the first public
school ever patronized was held, in 1652, and probably afterwards, as no school house was erected; in
which the five commissioners of the first court of
admiralty, organized in 1665 by Gov. Nicholls, con-
vened and held their sessions; and in which
during the civil war between the houses of

Bayard and Leisler, (our colonial York and Lancaster,) one party held possession, and returned the fire of his enemy at the fort. Here also in the winter season, many of the public balls were given, but when the "night watch" made its rounds all absent persons were warned to return to their homes. This famous edifice was owned or occupied about one hundred and eighteen years ago by Brinckerhoof and Van Wyck, and in 1806 by Abraham Brinckerhoof. The original building was of stone, but when late in the seventeenth century some changes were made, it presented a brick front.

Near the city hall was Slyk-steeg, Mire-lane; and a tannery extended from the north corner of the lane, passing from Coenties-slip to Mire-lane, on which a bark mill stood; hence the name of Mill street. In rear of this was elevated ground, and in close proximity was de Warmoes-straet (street of vegetables)—Garden street, near which were the Citizens' guard-house, and the *Luthersche Kerck*. The Lutherans, Jews and Quakers found very little toleration from the Dutch, but the English governors were more indulgent. In 1671 Gov. Lovelace authorized the Lutheran congregation to erect a church; and Edmundson from England was allowed to preach to the society of his order. At an inn he held the first "Friends meeting" in the city, and the magistrates attended. From Coenties-slip to Hanover-square was the Cingel, Encircling or Exterior street; thence from the Rondeel, which is now a part of Old slip, towards the Water-poort, was the burghers' or citizens' path. Near the Cingel commenced Smeer-straet (Greese street) or Smet-straet, afterwards called Smith street, and now the lower end of William street. The Block house at the water gate was at the northeast corner of the present Pearl and Wall streets. The stone wall connecting the *Ronduyten* was designed to keep out the inundation of the tide and sea. The city wall was of earth, thrown up from a moat dug in 1653 from the East to the North rivers, at first four or five feet deep and ten or eleven broad, somewhat sloping at the bottom. On the top of this wall was a closely connected line of palisadoes extending a like distance from the water gate along the north side of the street now called Wall street to the North river; hence was derived the name of Wall street, which coursed along the southern base of the moat, wall, and line of palisadoes. The water port or gate was connected with the block-house at the east end of the wall. The land-port, or city gate, was on Broadway, from thence the wall and palisadoes extended to a fortification in the rear of Trinity church.

This breast-work or battery, four or five feet thick, may have been the same stone wall, which in 1751 was discovered eight feet under ground in rear of the English church. The "Lady's Valley," a fashionable resort in the days of Gov.

Kieft, was probably the same place which was de-
nominated in the period of his successor "Maagde-
Paetje," (the Virgin's path,) now Maiden lane. It
was called Green lane in 1692, when the common
council ordered the land on the water side in front of
Smee's vly, from the Block house to the hill, now
called Beekman street, and that portion extending
from the Block house to Green lane, to be sold at
twenty shillings per foot. The Virgin's path pro-
ceeded from this Vly in the direction of Maiden
lane to the elevated ground. Smee's vly was a
marsh extending from the rising ground a little
north of the city walls, along the East river or shore
of Pearl street to the rising ground near Fulton
street. This valley, or salt marsh was bounded
westward by the high ground along the rear of the
lots on the northwestern side of Pearl street. The
Vly was spoken of as early as the time of Van Twiller. The English, adopting the sound without the
sense of the word, called it Fly. In 1676 the common council ordered the tan-vats and slaughter
houses to be removed out of the city and a public
slaughter house to be erected "over the water without
the gate at Smith's Fly, near the Half-Moon."
Asher Levy, in partnership with Garret Johnson
Rose, built the house and received a grant of its ex-
clusive use. This was the foundation of Rose's,
or the Fly-market."

North of the Vly and between Beeckman's hill

and Frankfort street was a waste wet piece of
ground known by the name of Beeckman's swamp.
Jacob street, and parts of Ferry, Gold and William
streets now cover it. This district of the city is
still known by the name of "the Swamp." North of
the rising ground that bounded Beeckman's swamp
was another but a much larger swamp meadow or
pond. It reached to the East river and was not completely filled in until 1794. It occupied the area of
parts of Cherry and Roosevelt streets, Batavia-lane,
James, Oliver, Catharine, Fayette streets and the
Jews'-alley to Chatham street, thence westward, it
communicated by a stream called the "fresh water river" with the fresh water pool or de Kolck. The city
also at this early period possessed a "Wint Molen"
(wind mill), erected in 1662, outside of the land
port, on the Company's farm in Broadway, between
Liberty and Cortlandt streets. The old wind-mill
having decayed, upon application made to the
governor and council, its builders received from the
authorities the stones and iron work of the mill on
condition that they should grind, gratis for the company, "twenty-five schepels" or nineteen bush-
els of corn per week, if so much should be wanted.
Beyond the Swamp-meadow on the East river was
Nechtant, the Indian name of Corlaer's-hook,
which has also been called Crown-point. Jacobus
Van Corlaer owned the property, and had a plan-
tation there in the time of Wouter Van Twiller.

He was Van Twiller's trumpeter. De Vriez records that on the 8th of August the first gunner of the fort gave a frolick. On one of the points of the fort a tent was erected, and tables and benches placed for the invited people. When the glee was at its highest, Corlaer the trumpeter began to blow, which occasioned a quarrel, and the Koopman of the stores, and the Koopman of the cargoes gave the trumpeter names. The trumpeter in revenge, gave them each a drubbing; when they ran home for their swords, and would take revenge of the trumpeter. Swaggering and boasting much they went to the house of the governor and would have eaten the trumpeter; but when the wine had evaporated in the morning, their courage was somewhat lowered, and they did not endeavor much to find the trumpeter." In 1652 Van Corlaer sold his property to William Beeckman for the sum of £750. West of Corlaer's-hook was the "Bouwerie" or farm, which in 1651 Gov. Stuyvesant purchased with a dwelling house, barn, reeklands, six cows, two horses, and two young negroes, for sixty-four hundred guilders (£1066.13,4.)

Bryant locates the place near Tenth street, a little east of Third avenue.

The general appearance of the city was attractive, rendered so to a great extent by the numerous orchards, gardens, arbors, pleasure grounds, and forest trees which shaded it. Its aspect was diversified by hill and dale, and its eminences were clustered with buildings; the whole forming a most delightful perspective from the water.

The Flats, covering the site of the city hall and its park, were favorite resorts of the burghers and their English fellow-townsmen. Then came the farms and the "bouwerie," from which the present Bowery takes its name.

The out-door amusements of the people in the day-time were varied in their character, and much time was spent on the ice; for the two rivers and the bay were covered with ice more frequently than now. Men, women and children glided swiftly on skates from point to point, and many of them bore upon their heads the produce of their Dutch farms.

Brodhead says that in the summer season the trees of the virgin soil about New York yielded a bountiful supply of peaches, and strawberries were to be found in great abundance. Excursions were frequently made to gather them, on which occasions the girls and boys, loaded with rich cream and sugar, resorted to the fields and there spent many happy hours.

The people from the villages further north near the Sound reached New York usually by water, deeming the perils of Hell-Gate safer than the woods in which lurked hidden dangers. Residents of the town desiring to reach Long Island at its nearest point summoned a ferryman, by blowing a horn which hung upon the branch of a tree near the landing. The ferryman's boat would carry them over to *Brenkelen*. Denton describes Brooklyn as a village with a small and ugly church standing in the middle of the road, whence the traveler might find his way as best he could to Vlacke-Bos, (Flat-bush); to Rust-dorp, (Jamaica); and to the more distant hamlets.

The pages of Knickerbocker's history picture the homes of the early Dutch colonists as being places where hospitality was boundless; and where the Hollander sat by his large tiled fire-place with his long clay pipe in hand. The floor about him was sprinkled with clean, white sand, and the low studded room was scrupulously clean. Over the Dutch gable of his house swung the traditional weather-cock, and upon the *stoep* the family collected during the warm summer evenings.

The farm of Dominie Bogardus, called the *Dominie's Bouwerie*, the Duke's farm, the King's farm, the Queen's farm, as it passed from one owner to another, became at length the property of Trinity church by letters-patent under the seal of the province.

O'Callaghan notes the fact that to the conveyance of this farm to Gov. Lovelace in 1671 by the children of Anetje Jans, (the widow of Dominie Bogardus,) one of the sons was not a party, and therefore the property is claimed by his descendants.

Bryant, in his history of the United States, gives an incident relating to Dominie Bogardus, showing that he did not always exercise that forbearance and gentleness which clergymen are supposed usually to possess. Van Twiller's administration had brought upon himself the contempt of the people, and had kept the little band of officials in continual perplexity. The incompetent governor had become more and more imbecile in his management of home affairs, and he was continually involved in petty quarrels with his associates. On one occasion Dominie Bogardus called him "a child of the devil," and declared that he would give him "such a shake from the pulpit on the next Sunday, that would make him shudder." No doubt the governor deserved it, for he often brought disgrace upon himself and his office, by brawling over his wine with drunken superintendents or captains, among whom he found congenial companionship.

In concluding this brief record it may be well to observe that, according to Stevens, it was the Protestant Commonwealth of England which passed the Navigation Act of 1660, directed against the foreign trade of her growing rival of the same religious faith. In this act may be found the germ of the policy of England not only toward her neighbors, but also toward her colonies. This act was maintained in force after the restoration of Charles II to the throne. Enforced at home, it was evaded in the British American colonies. The arm of England was long, but her hand lay lightly on the American continent, for the extent of coast and frontier was too great to be watched, and the English neighbors of the Dutch in Maryland and Virginia conducted much illicit trade with them. In 1663 the losses to the revenue were so great that the men who enjoyed a monopoly from the King entered complaints and stated that the interest of the kingdom was at stake, and therefore the conquest of the New Netherland was resolved upon.

In Winsor's Narrative and Critical History of America we read that it is the fashion of historians to ascribe the seizure of New Netherland to the perfidity of Charles; but the policy of kingdoms through successive administrations is more homogenous than appears on the surface. The diplomacy of ministers is traditional; and the opportunity which seems to make a change is often but an incident in the chain. That which presented itself to Clarendon was the demand made by the States-General that the boundary line should be established between the Dutch and the English possessions in America. Consent on the part of Charles would have been a ratification of Cromwell's recognition of 1654. This demand of the Dutch government made in 1664 precipitated the crisis. The seizure of New Amsterdam, the reduction of New Netherland was resolved upon, and in February,

1664, an expedition was ordered against the Dutch in America. James Duke of York, grand admiral, was the heir to the crown, and a patent to him from the King his brother would merge therein; and an authority established over the territory covered by this grant might with limitations be extended over the colonies. In this scheme may be found the beginning in America of that policy of personal rule, which, begun under the Catholic Stuart, culminated under the Protestant Hanoverian a century later, in the oppression which brought on the American Revolution.

Truly is it said that the Dutch settlers landed on Manhattan Island with the minister and school master, and founded not only the first fully organized church but also the first day school in the United States. These Hollanders provided schools for the education of their own children as well as for the benefit of the Indians, and the people of other nationalities sojourning among them. Years before John Eliot began preaching to the aboriginees the dominies from Holland instructed Indian converts in Christianity, whose names are still to be seen in many a church register on Manhattan Island. In New York the Dutchmen kept up the fight for freedom in religion for one hundred and thirteen years, never yielding until finally in 1777 it was secured in the constitution of the Empire state, and thus leading all the states in the catholic spirit which ultimately became the supreme law of the land.

Chronological Data.

1609 Hudson discovers the river named after him.

1614 The New Netherland Company receives its charter.

1618 Expiration of the first New Netherland charter.

1621 The Dutch West India Company incorporated.

1622 The Dutch West India Company takes formal possession of New Netherland.

1623 Walloon emigration to New Netherland.

1624 Cornelis Jacobsen May, Governor of New Netherland.

1625 William Verhult, Governor of New Netherland.

1626 Peter Minuit, Governor of New Netherland.

1629 Issue of the Charter of Privileges and Exemptions by the Dutch West India Co.

1631 Peter Minuit recalled.

1633 Wouter Van Twiller, Governor of New Netherland.

1637 Van Twiller recalled.

1638 William Kieft, Governor of New Netherland.

1647 Peter Stuyvesant arrives at New Amsterdam as Governor of New Netherland.

1653 Elective municipal government established at New Amsterdam.

1664 Grant of New Netherland to the Duke of York, and its surrender to the English—Named New York.

1668 Lovelace, Governor of New York.

1673 Recapture of New York by the Dutch.

1674 Treaty of Westminster confirms New York to the English.

1674 Andros, Governor of New York.

1680 Brockholst, Lieutenant-governor of New York.

1683 Dongon, Governor of New York.

1683 First Popular Assembly in New York.

1689 Nicholson, Lieutenant-governor of New York.

1689 Usurpation of the government by Liesler.

1691 Sloughter, Governor of New York.

1691 Execution of Liesler.

1692 Fletcher, Governor of New York

1696 The first Trinity Church erected.

1696 Kidd sails from New York.

1698 Bellomont, Governor of New York, Massachusetts, and New Hampshire.

1702 Cornbury, Governor of New York and New Jersey.

1708 Lovelace, Governor of New York.

1710 Hunter, Governor of New York.

1712 The negroes rose in insurrection.

1720 Burnet, Governor of New York.

1725 Bradford established the New York Gazette.

1728 Montgomerie, Governor of New York.

1729 A City Library was founded.

1732 Cosby, Governor of New York.

1736 Clarke, Lieutenant governor of New York.

1740 The New York Society Library organized.

1741 "Negro Plot" in New York.

1743 Clinton, Governor of New York.

1750 A theatre was estalished.

1753 De Lancey, Governor of New York.

1754 King's (now Columbia) College was chartered.

1773 Sandy Hook lighthouse first lighted.

1765 Meeting of the First Continental Congress, known as the "Stamp Act Congress"
at the Old City Hall, Wall street, New York.

1766 News of the repeal of the act received in the city.

1768 Chamber of Commerce was organized at the Queen's Head Tavern, known
later as Fraunces' Tavern, located on the corner of Pearl and Broad streets.

1770 Lead statue of George III set up in Bowling Green.

1770 A statue of Wm. Pitt was erected corner Wall and William streets.

1776 Arrival of British Fleet in New York Bay.

1776 (April 14) Washington arrives at New York.

1776 (July 4) Declaration of Independence by Congress.

1776 (Aug. 6) The British take possession.

1776 (Sept. 15) Americans abandon New York.

1776 (Sept. 21) Burning of New York; 492 houses destroyed.

1777 New York adopts a Constitution.

1777 Flag of Stars and Stripes adopted by Congress.

1778   Commissioners sent to Congress by Lord North with Proposals for Peace

1783   (Nov. 25) The British evacuated the city, and Gen. Washington entered it at the head of the American army.

1783   (Dec. 4) Washington takes leave of his officers at the close of the Revolution, at his headquarters, corner of Pearl and Broad streets.

1783   (Dec. 23) Resignation of General Washington.

1785   Congress removed from Philadelphia to New York, and met in the City Hall corner Wall and Nassau streets.

1785   The Bank of New York was organized.

1788   New Constitution of the United States was adopted.

1789   (March 4) First Congress assembled in New York.

1789   (April 30) Washington was inaugurated first President of the United States, in front of the old City Hall, facing Broad street.

1789   The New Federal Constitution was ratified.

1792   The Tontine Coffee-house was built.

1795   The Park Theatre was erected.

1797   Capital transferred from New York to Albany.

1799   The Manhattan Company was chartered to supply the city with water.

1801   New York Evening Post established.

1804   Hackney coaches were first licensed.

1805   The New York Free School incorporated.

1805   Organization of the Tammany Society

1806   Steam navigation introduced by Fulton. Trip made from New York to Albany in 32 hours; returning in 30 hours.

1807   City surveyed and laid out by Gouverneur Morris, De Witt Clinton and others

1809   First woolen mills started in New York.

1812   Declaration of war against Great Britain.

1812   First steam ferry to Jersey City.

1814   Suspension of specie payments, which lasted till July, 1817.

1815   First news of the treaty of peace received.

1823   First gas company organized in New York.

1824   Gen. La Fayette arrived in the city.

1825   Gas was first introduced and mains laid in Broadway.

1825   The quintal of 100 instead of 112 pounds was adopted as the new measure.

1825   Erie Canal opened for traffic.

1825   Departure of La Fayette for France.

1826   (Oct. 26) Erie Canal completed, and the lakes thus united with the Atlantic.

1826   (Nov. 11) Arrival of the first boat by the Erie Canal

1832   Asiatic cholera ravaged the city.

1832   University of New York organized.

1835   New York Herald established.

1835 Great conflagration, which raged three days and destroyed more than 600 buildings.

1836-7 Great financial panic, and banks suspend specie payments.

1339 Specie payments resumed.

1841 The New York Tribune established.

1842 The Croton Aqueduct was completed.

1845 Another disastrous fire in the city, in which 300 buildings were burned.

1846 California expedition, under Stephenson, sails from New York.

1849 The Astor Place riot.

1851 Ovation to Kossuth, the Hungarian patriot.

1852 First street railway in New York.

1853 Crystal Palace opened in a structure of iron and glass placed on Reservoir square.

1853 Yellow Fever in New York.

1853 Children's Aid Society founded at New York.

1855 Central Park selected by commissioners appointed by the Supreme Conrt.

1856 Republican party formed.

1857 Great financial crisis; banks suspend Oct. 14-15; resume specie payments Dec. 12-14.

1858 Atlantic Cable celebration.

1859 Arrival at New York of the Great Eastern, June 28.

1860 Arrival of the Japanese embassy.

1860 Visit of the Prince of Wales.

1860 Secession of South Carolina.

1861 Attack upon Fort Sumter.

1861 Banks suspend specie payments.

1863 (July 13, 14, 15) Anti-draft riots in New York; furions attacks upon the negro population; 2000 rioters killed.

1864 New York Sanitary Commission Fair, receipts over one milliou dollars.

1864 Gold reaches highest premium, viz, 284 per cent., July 16.

1865 Assassinatiou of President Lincoln.

1866 Emma, Queen of the Sandwich Islands, visits New York.

1869 (Sept. 24) Great Wall street panic.

1872 The citizens combined against the public plunderers, and the leaders of the Ring brought to justice.

1873 Another financial crash. (Black Friday.)

1878 Chinese Embassy visits New York.

1878 (Dec. 17) Gold sold at par—the first time since 1862.

1879 (Jan. 1) Resumptiou of specie payments.

1881 Revised New Testameut published.

1883 (May 24) Opening of the Brooklyn Suspension Bridge.

1884   Departure from New York of the Greely relief steamers "Bear" and "Thetis."

1884   Great panic in Wall street.

1884   Corner stone laid of the Bartholdi Statue of Liberty.

1885   Revised Old Testament and complete Bible published.

1885   Flood Rock successfully blown up.

1888   (June 4-7.)   The first International Congress of Anthropology met at Columbia College, under the auspices of the New York Academy of Anthropology.   Prince Roland Bonaparte, Vice-Pres., in attendance.

1889   (*In futuro*).   April 30th, Centennial Celebration of the Inauguration of General George Washington as President of the United States.